THE I SPY AND LEARN DINOSAURS

ALPHABET BOOK

Ages 2+

Copyright © 2021 by Monét McNally

Please note the information contained within this document is for educational and entertainment purposes only. All effort has been executed to present accurate, up-to-date and reliable information. The content has been derived from various sources as listed on the reference pages.

Hi there!

I am excited for you to begin your dinosaur adventure. I hope you find it to be entertaining, fun and educational!

And if you like this book, let us know by heading over to Amazon and writing a quick review! Reviews provide great feedback and help other readers like yourself decide whether or not they would enjoy this book, too.

Thank you for your support and I hope you enjoy!

ARE YOU READY FOR YOUR
I SPY DINOSAURS ADVENTURE?

LET'S BEGIN!

NEED A REFRESHER?

CHECK OUT THE
A TO Z LIST OF
DINOSAUR NAMES
FOUND AT THE END.

I SPY with my little eye something that starts with...

A

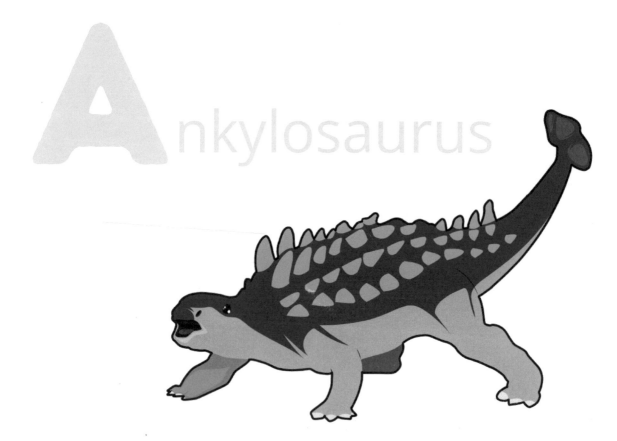

Ankylosaurus

an-KIE-loh-sore-us

Name Meaning: Ankylosaurus means "stiff lizard"
   Why? Bones in its skull and body were fused together which provided strength[8]

Diet: plants

Interesting Fact: Its back had thick, protective bony knobs that are commonly found in crocodiles today[18]

I SPY with my little eye something that starts with...

Brachiosaurus

BRAK-ee-oh-sore-us

Name Meaning: Brachiosaurus means "arm lizard"

Why? It had a very long neck and tail. It was around 39 feet tall (twice the height of an adult male giraffe)

Diet: plants

Interesting Fact: An adult brachiosaurus weighed about 80 tons (equal to the weight of 13 elephants combined)[2]

I SPY with my little eye something that starts with...

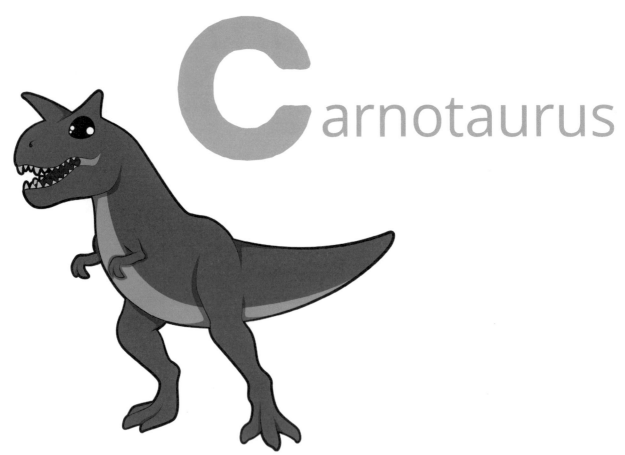

Carnotaurus

Kar-noh-TORE-us

Name Meaning: Carnotaurus means "meat-eating bull"
Why? It had thick bull-like horns on the top of its head [6]

Diet: meat

Interesting Fact: It looked like a T. rex with horns, but its arms were smaller than the arms of a T. rex [29]

I SPY with my little eye something that starts with...

D

Dilophosaurus

dye-LOAF-oh-sore-us

Name Meaning: Dilophosaurus means "two-crested lizard"
Why? It had two thin and bony crests on top of its head

Diet: meat

Interesting Fact: The Dilophosaurus was not small as seen in films; it was over 20 feet tall and weighed around 1,000 pounds[7]

I SPY with my little eye something that starts with...

E

Edmontonia

ed-mon-TONE-ee-ah

Name Meaning: Edmontonia means "of Edmonton"
Why? Its fossils were found in a unit of rock known as the Edmonton Formation

Diet: plants

Interesting Fact: When threatened, it would crouch down on the ground to protect its soft and defenseless underbelly[13]

I SPY with my little eye something that starts with... F

F ukuisaurus

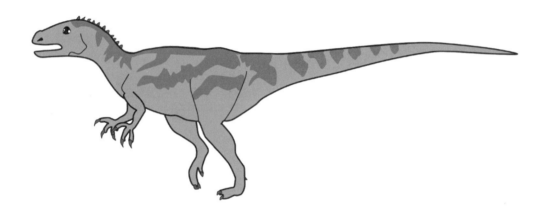

foo-koo-l-sore-us

Name Meaning: Fukuisaurus means "Fukui lizard"
   Why? Its fossils were found in the Fukui Prefecture (district) of
   Japan

Diet: plants

Interesting Fact: It had long and sharp, curved claws on its
hands that were similar to the Velociraptor's deadly foot claw [39]

I SPY with my little eye something that starts with...

Gallimimus

gal-lee-MEEM-us

Name Meaning: Gallimimus means "chicken mimic"
Why? It resembled a flightless bird [16]

Diet: meat and plants

Interesting Fact: This ostrich–like dinosaur was one of the fastest dinosaurs in history; it could run up to 60 km/h (37 mph) [26]

I SPY with my little eye something that starts with... H

Huayangosaurus

hoy-YANG-oh-SORE-us

Name Meaning: Huayangosaurus means "Huayang lizard"
Why? Its fossils were found in Huayang, China

Diet: plants

Interesting Fact: It had blood vessels in the bony plates on its back that allowed the plates to change color to deter predators or attract mates[24]

I SPY with my little eye something that starts with...

I

Iguanodon

ig-WHA-noh-don

Name Meaning: Iguanodon means "iguana tooth"
  Why? Its teeth were similar to the teeth of iguanas today

Diet: plants

Interesting Fact: It had thumb spikes on its hands that were used for protection and food preparation[25]

I SPY with my little eye something that starts with...

J

Juravenator

ju-rah-ve-nay-tor

Name Meaning: Juravenator means "Jura hunter"

Why? It was a meat–eating dinosaur whose fossils were found in the Jura Mountains in Germany[23]

Diet: meat

Interesting Fact: They were nocturnal so they were most active during the night[27]

I SPY with my little eye something that starts with...

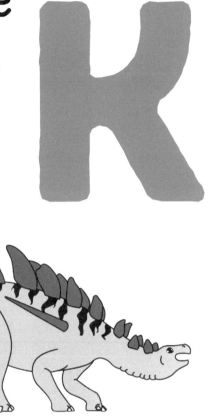

Kentrosaurus

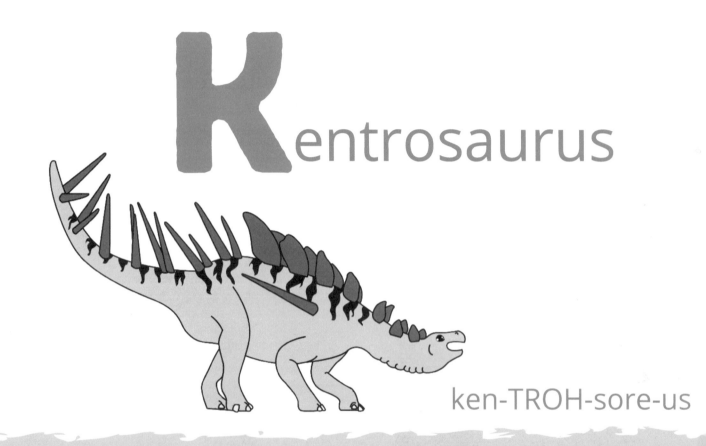

ken-TROH-sore-us

Name Meaning: Kentrosaurus means "spiky lizard"

Why? It had two rows of spikes along its back and tail; it also had two large spikes on its front shoulders

Diet: plants

Interesting Fact: With a motion speed of over 40 meters per second (around 1.2 times faster than a hurricane), its powerful spiked tail could slash through body tissue and shatter bones [21]

I SPY with my little eye something that starts with...

Lambeosaurus

lam-BEE-oh-SORE-us

Name Meaning: Lambeosaurus means "lambe's lizard"
   Why? It was named after the paleontologist Lawrence Lambe
   whom discovered it [3]

Diet: plants

Interesting Fact: The bony crest on the top of its head could change colors to communicate with other members in the herd [31]

I SPY with my little eye something that starts with...

M

Microraptor

MIKE-row-rap-tor

Name Meaning: Microraptor means "small thief"

Why? It was a meat-eating dinosaur that was only about 1 meter long (around the length of a baseball bat)[20]

Diet: meat

Interesting Fact: It had four wings because it had long feathers on both its arms and both its legs[22, 38]

I SPY with my little eye something that starts with...

N

Nodosaurus

no-doh-SORE-us

Name Meaning: Nodosaurus means "node lizard"
   Why? It was an armored dinosaur that looked like a gigantic horned toad

Diet: plants

Interesting Fact: Compared to other armored dinosaurs, its skull was not covered by protective plates, and it did not have a club on its tail[4]

I SPY with my little eye something that starts with...

Oviraptor

OH-vee-RAP-tor

Name Meaning: Oviraptor means "egg thief"

Why? Scientists suggested that its fossils were found on a pile of stolen *Protoceratops* eggs; later, this was proven to be false because the eggs were *Oviraptor* eggs [33]

Diet: meat and plants

Interesting Fact: It was the world's first preserved dinosaur to be found on a nest of eggs filled with fossilized babies [30]

I SPY with my little eye something that starts with...

P

Pachycephalosaurus

pack-i-KEF-al-oh-sore-russ

Name Meaning: Pachycephalosaurus means "thick-headed lizard"

Why? It had a dome shaped skull on top of its head

Diet: plants

Interesting Fact: The skull roof on its head was about 10 inches thick (30 times thicker than a human skull)[1]

I SPY with my little eye something that starts with...

Q

Quaesitosaurus

kwee-siet-oh-sore-us

Name Meaning: Quaesitosaurus means "extraordinary lizard"
Why? It had a very long neck and a tail that was like a whip[28]

Diet: plants

Interesting Fact: It would swallow small mineral rocks (called gastroliths) because the stones helped grind up food in its stomach[11]

I SPY with my little eye something that starts with...

Rugops

roo-gops

Name Meaning: Rugops means "wrinkle face"
Why? It had bulging blood vessels along its head that looked like wrinkles

Diet: meat

Interesting Fact: It was a 30-foot long creature that looked like a T. rex but it did not have large teeth[35]

I SPY with my little eye something that starts with...

S

Spinosaurus

SPINE-oh-SORE-us

Name Meaning: Spinosaurus means "spine lizard"
   Why? It had a large bony fin on its back about 5.4 feet long[9]

Diet: meat

Interesting Fact: It was the largest meat–eating dinosaur with a length of up to 59 feet (the length of one big rig trailer)[12]

I SPY with my little eye something that starts with...

T

ROAR!

Tyrannosaurus rex

tie-RAN-oh-sore-us rex

Name Meaning: T. rex means "king of the tyrant lizards"
Why? It had the largest teeth of any dinosaur at 12 inches; it also had the strongest bite of any land animal in Earth's[10] history

Diet: meat

Interesting Fact: Its bite was so powerful that it was equal to the force of a large African elephant sitting down (or twice as strong as a crocodile bite)[15]

I SPY with my little eye something that starts with...

Utahraptor

YOO-tah-RAP-tor

Name Meaning: Utahraptor means "Utah thief"
  Why? It was a hunter known to prey on large dinosaurs and its
  fossils were found in Utah

Diet: meat

Interesting Fact: It was the largest of all raptor dinosaurs (larger
than a velociraptor)[34]

I SPY with my little eye something that starts with...

Velociraptor

vel-OSS-ee-rap-tor

Name Meaning: Velociraptor means "speedy thief"
Why? It was a meat–eating dinosaur that could run about 40 mph (60 kph)

Diet: meat

Interesting Fact: Researchers described them to be similar to modern day eagles because they had feathers, and their claws resembled the talons of an eagle [19]

I SPY with my little eye something that starts with...

Wendiceratops

WEN-dee-CERE-ah-TOPS

Name Meaning: Wendiceratops means "Wendy's horned-face"
Why? It was a member of the horned dinosaur family and its fossils were discovered by fossil hunter, Wendy Sloboda[32]

Diet: plants

Interesting Fact: It is the only dinosaur to have a skull surrounded by curled horns that looked like hooks[14]

I SPY with my little eye something that starts with...

X

Xenoceratops

ZEE-no-SEH-rah-tops

Name Meaning: Xenoceratops means "alien horned-face"
  Why? It had a strange pattern of horns on its head; also, horned dinosaurs' fossils were rarely found in this location

Diet: meat

Interesting Fact: It measured around 20 feet (6 meters) long and weighed more than 2 tons (similar to the weight of a rhinoceros)[5]

I SPY with my little eye something that starts with...

Y

Y inlong

yin-long

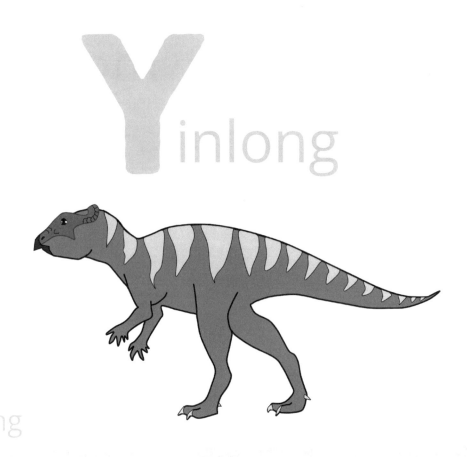

Name Meaning: Yinlong means "hidden dragon"

Why? Its fossils were found near the location the movie Crouching Tiger, Hidden Dragon (2000) was filmed[37]

Diet: plants

Interesting Fact: It had large canine-like teeth at the front of its beak that were used for eating and to defend itself[17]

I SPY with my little eye something that starts with...

Z

Zephyrosaurus

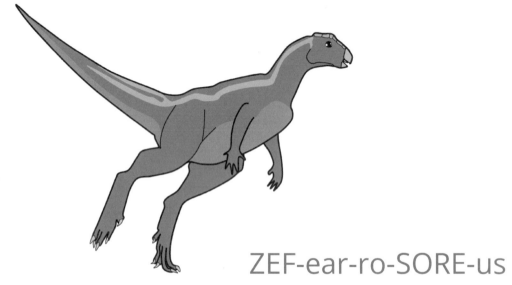

ZEF-ear-ro-SORE-us

Name Meaning: Zephyrosaurus means "westward wind lizard" *Why?* It was named after a Greek deity [40]

Diet: plants

Interesting Fact: It was a burrowing dinosaur; it would make holes to find food, avoid predators or escape harsh weather conditions [36]

A-Z LIST OF
DINOSAUR NAMES

ALPHABET DINOSAURS

Ankylosaurus

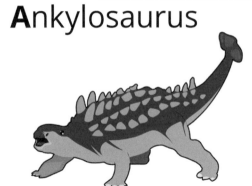

Brachiosaurus

Carnotaurus

Dilophosaurus

Edmontonia

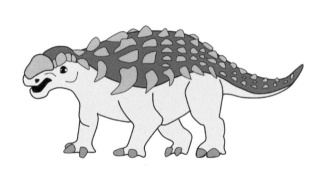

Fukuisaurus

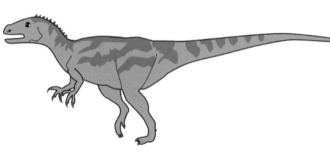

Gallimimus

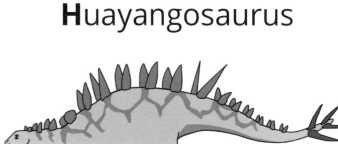

Huayangosaurus

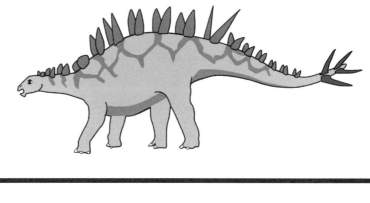

Iguanodon

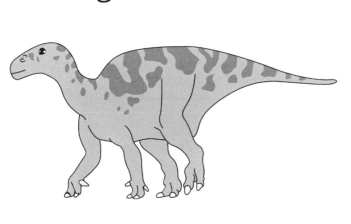

Juravenator

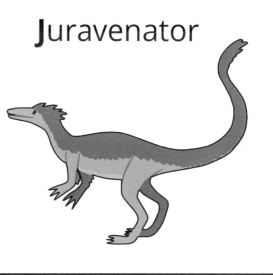

Kentrosaurus

Lambeosaurus

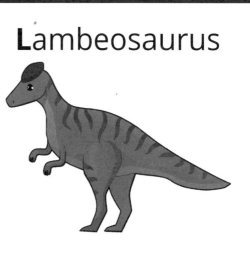

Microraptor

Nodosaurus

Oviraptor

Pachycephalosaurus

Quaesitosaurus

Rugops

Spinosaurus

Tyrannosaurus rex

Utahraptor

Velociraptor

Wendiceratops

Xenoceratops

Yinlong

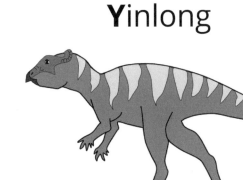

Zephyrosaurus

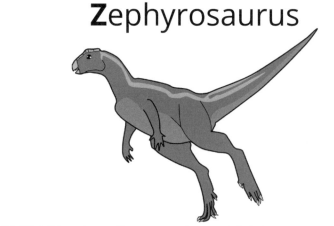

OTHER DINOSAURS YOU MAY SEE

Andesaurus

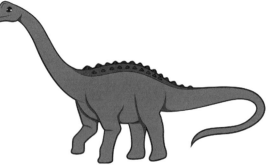

Baryonyx

Coelophysis

Diplodocus

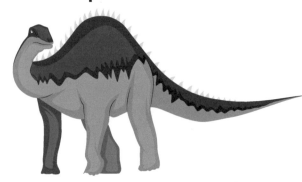

Europasaurus

Parasaurolophus

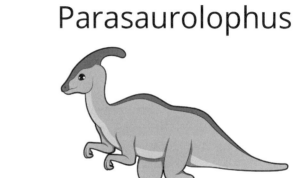

Stegosaurus

Styracosaurus

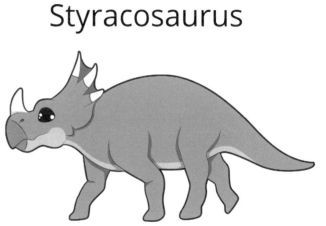

Tsintaosaurus

You Made It!

I hope you enjoyed your I spy dinosaurs adventure and learned tons of fun facts along the way. I look forward to seeing you again on our next I spy adventure.

Interested in other cool books?

Get a FREE digital sample of *The I Spy and Search Dinosaurs Seek and Find Book*.

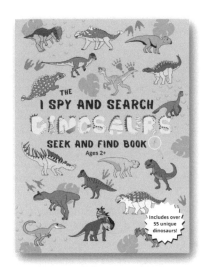

To **DOWNLOAD**, click on the link below or scan the QR code to get your freebie today!

https://pages.mmcreativepublishing.com/freebie

References

1. Allmon, W. D., and D. S. Friend, 2015, Fossils of the Northwest central uS. pages 81–141, in: M. D. Lucas, r. M. ross, & a. N. Swaby (eds.). The Teacher-Friendly Guide to the Earth Science of the Northwest Central US. paleontological research Institution, Ithaca, New York.

2. Britannica, T. Editors of Encyclopaedia (2019, February 26). brachiosaur. Encyclopedia Britannica. https://www.britannica.com/animal/brachiosaur

3. Britannica, T. Editors of Encyclopaedia (2019, February 22). Lambeosaurus. Encyclopedia Britannica. https://www.britannica.com/animal/Lambeosaurus

4. Britannica, T. Editors of Encyclopaedia (2017, November 23). Nodosaurus. Encyclopedia Britannica. https://www.britannica.com/animal/Nodosaurus

5. Canadian Science Publishing (NRC Research Press). (2012, November 8). Meet Xenoceratops: Canada's newest horned dinosaur. ScienceDaily. Retrieved December 20, 2021 from www.sciencedaily.com/releases/2012/11/121108074008.htm

6. Carnotaurus. Days of the Dinosaur: Dino Battle Exhibit. Science Museum of Minnesota. (n.d.). Retrieved December 22, 2021, from https://new.smm.org/dino-days/battle/carnotaurus

7. Carter, N. (2019, April 23). The Real Dilophosaurus. Philip J. Currie Dinosaur Museum. Retrieved December 22, 2021, from https://dinomuseum.ca/2019/04/23/the-real-dilophosaurus/

8. Castro, J. (2017, May 10). Ankylosaurus: Facts about the armored lizard. LiveScience. Retrieved December 22, 2021, from https://www.livescience.com/25222-ankylosaurus.html

9. Castro, J. (2016, March 18). Spinosaurus: The largest carnivorous dinosaur. LiveScience. Retrieved December 22, 2021, from https://www.livescience.com/24120-spinosaurus.html

0. Castro, J. (2017, October 17). Tyrannosaurus rex: King of the dinosaurs. LiveScience. Retrieved December 22, 2021, from https://www.livescience.com/23868-tyrannosaurus-rex-facts.html

11. Chatterjee, S., & Zheng, Z. (2002). Cranial anatomy of Shunosaurus, a basal sauropod dinosaur from the Middle Jurassic of China. Zoological Journal of the Linnean Society, 136, 145-169.

12. Culotta, E. (2014, September 11). This is the only known swimming dinosaur. Science. Retrieved December 22, 2021, from https://www.science.org/content/article/only-known-swimming-dinosaur

13. "Edmontonia." In: Dodson, Peter & Britt, Brooks & Carpenter, Kenneth & Forster, Catherine A. & Gillette, David D. & Norell, Mark A. & Olshevsky, George & Parrish, J. Michael & Weishampel, David B. The Age of Dinosaurs. Publications International, LTD. p. 141. ISBN 0-7853-0443-6.

14. Evans DC, Ryan MJ (2015) Cranial Anatomy of Wendiceratops pinhornensis gen. et sp. nov., a Centrosaurine Ceratopsid (Dinosauria: Ornithischia) from the Oldman Formation (Campanian), Alberta, Canada, and the Evolution of Ceratopsid Nasal Ornamentation. PLoS ONE 10(7): e0130007. https://doi.org/10.1371/journal.pone.0130007

15. Fortner, J., Wilken, A., Sellers, K., Cost, I., Middleton, K. and Holliday, C. (2021), The Role of the Intramandibular Joint, Symphyseal Tissues, and Wrapping Muscles on Theropod Dinosaur Mandibular Function. The FASEB Journal, 35:. https://doi.org/10.1096/fasebj.2021.35.S1.03068

16. Gallimimus. The Natural History Museum. (n.d.). Retrieved December 22, 2021, from https://www.nhm.ac.uk/discover/dino-directory/gallimimus.html

17. HAN, F.-L., FORSTER, C. A., CLARK, J. M., & XU, X. (2016). CRANIAL ANATOMY OF YINLONG DOWNSI (ORNITHISCHIA: CERATOPSIA) FROM THE UPPER JURASSIC SHISHUGOU FORMATION OF XINJIANG, CHINA. Journal of Vertebrate Paleontology, 36(1), 1–27. http://www.jstor.org/stable/24740230

18. Hayashi, S., Carpenter, K., Scheyer, T.M., Watabe, M., & Suzuki, D. (2010). Function and Evolution of Ankylosaur Dermal Armor.

19. Hendry, L. (n.d.). Vicious velociraptor: Tales of a Turkey-sized dinosaur. Natural History Museum. Retrieved December 22, 2021, from https://www.nhm.ac.uk/discover/velociraptor-facts.html

20. Hone DWE, Tischlinger H, Xu X, Zhang F (2010) The Extent of the Preserved Feathers on the Four-Winged Dinosaur Microraptor gui under Ultraviolet Light. PLoS ONE 5(2): e9223. https://doi.org/10.1371/journal.pone.0009223

21. Mallison, H. (2011). Defense capabilities of Kentrosaurus aethiopicus Hennig, 1915 Palaeontogia Electronica

22. *Microraptor*. The Natural History Museum. (n.d.). Retrieved December 22, 2021, from https://www.nhm.ac.uk/discover/dino-directory/microraptor.html

23. Musmarra, N. and Lomax, D. R. (2012). Germany - Fossil of the Year 2009 - *Juravenator starki*: Dressed for Hunting. *Paleo Nature*. Multilingual Natural History Magazine, https://www.paleonature.org/educational/187-germany-fossil-of-the-year-2009-juravenator

24. New South Wales Government. (2020, November 25). Dinosaurs - *huayangosaurus taibaii*. The Australian Museum. Retrieved December 22, 2021, from https://australian.museum/learn/dinosaurs/fact-sheets/huayangosaurus-taibaii/

25. Osterloff, E. (n.d.). *Iguanodon: The teeth that led to a dinosaur discovery*. Natural History Museum. Retrieved December 22, 2021, from https://www.nhm.ac.uk/discover/the-discovery-of-iguanodon.html

26. Paul, G. (2001). LIMB DESIGN , FUNCTION AND RUNNING PERFORMANCE IN OSTRICH-MIMICS AND TYRANNOSAURS.

27. Phil R. Bell, Christophe Hendrickx, Crocodile-like sensory scales in a Late Jurassic theropod dinosaur, Current Biology, Volume 30, Issue 19, 2020, Pages R1068-R1070, ISSN 0960-9822, https://doi.org/10.1016/j.cub.2020.08.066. (https://www.sciencedirect.com/science/article/pii/S0960982220312562)

28. *Quaesitosaurus*. The Natural History Museum. (n.d.). Retrieved December 22, 2021, from https://www.nhm.ac.uk/discover/dino-directory/quaesitosaurus.html

29. RUIZ, J., TORICES, A., SERRANO, H. and LÓPEZ, V. (2011), The hand structure of *Carnotaurus sastrei* (Theropoda, Abelisauridae): implications for hand diversity and evolution in abelisaurids. Palaeontology, 54: 1271-1277. https://doi.org/10.1111/j.1475-4983.2011.01091.x

30. Shundong Bi, Romain Amiot, Claire Peyre de Fabrègues, Michael Pittman, Matthew C. Lamanna, Yilun Yu, Congyu Yu, Tzuruei Yang, Shukang Zhang, Qi Zhao, Xing Xu, An oviraptorid preserved atop an embryo-bearing egg clutch sheds light on the reproductive biology of non-avialan theropod dinosaurs, Science Bulletin, Volume 66, Issue 9, 2021, Pages 947-954, ISSN 2095-9273, https://doi.org/10.1016/j.scib.2020.12.018. (https://www.sciencedirect.com/science/article/pii/S2095927320307635)

31. Strauss, Bob. (2021, February 16). 10 Facts About Lambeosaurus, the Hatchet-Crested Dinosaur. Retrieved from https://www.thoughtco.com/lambeosaurus-the-hatchet-crested-dinosaur-1093809

32. The Cleveland Museum of Natural History. (2015, July 8). *Wendiceratops Pinhornensis New Horned Dinosaur Discovery*. Cleveland Museum of Natural History. Retrieved December 22, 2021, from https://www.cmnh.org/wendiceratops

33. The San Diego Natural History Museum. (n.d.). Dino Jaws Information Sheets for Educators and Students [Fact Sheet]. https://www.sdnhm.org/download_file/view/2417/479/

34. The University of Utah, ZapIsYou.Org Salt Lake County. (2021, August 12). *Utahraptor Ostrommaysorum*. Natural History Museum of Utah. Retrieved December 22, 2021, from https://nhmu.utah.edu/utahraptor-ostrommaysorum

35. University Of Chicago. (2004, June 9). Two Dinosaurs From Africa Give Clues To Continents' Split. *ScienceDaily*. Retrieved December 19, 2021 from www.sciencedaily.com/releases/2004/06/040609071516.htm

36. Varricchio, D. J., Martin, A. J., & Katsura, Y. (2007). First trace and body fossil evidence of a burrowing, denning dinosaur. *Proceedings. Biological sciences*, 274(1616), 1361–1368. https://doi.org/10.1098/rspb.2006.0443

37. Werning, S. (2013, August 29). *Yinlong. Encyclopedia Britannica*. https://www.britannica.com/animal/Yinlong

38. *When did dinosaurs become birds? evolution of flight: AMNH*. Dinosaurs Among Us. American Museum of Natural History. (n.d.). Retrieved December 22, 2021, from https://www.amnh.org/exhibitions/dinosaurs-among-us/flight

39. Yoichi Azuma and Philip J Currie. A new carnosaur (Dinosauria: Theropoda) from the Lower Cretaceous of Japan. Canadian Journal of Earth Sciences. 37(12): 1735-1753. https://doi.org/10.1139/e00-064

40. *Zephyrosaurus*. The Natural History Museum. (n.d.). Retrieved December 22, 2021, from https://www.nhm.ac.uk/discover/dino-directory/zephyrosaurus.html

Manufactured by Amazon.ca
Bolton, ON

30640673R00042